Small pets

Joyce Pope

Illustrated by
John Francis and Gary Hincks

SCIMITAR 90 Great Russell Street, London WC1B 3PT

Suitable pets

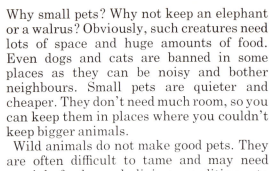

Rabbit

Why small pets? Why not keep an elephant or a walrus? Obviously, such creatures need lots of space and huge amounts of food. Even dogs and cats are banned in some places as they can be noisy and bother neighbours. Small pets are quieter and cheaper. They don't need much room, so you can keep them in places where you couldn't keep bigger animals.

Wild animals do not make good pets. They are often difficult to tame and may need special foods and living conditions to survive. The best sorts of pets are those which have been bred in captivity.

There are plenty of small animals that make good pets. If you do not own a garden, don't choose animals which prefer to live outdoors, like the ones below. Those on the right are more suited to life indoors.

Tortoise

Guinea pig

Gerbil

Budgerigar

Goldfish

Mouse

Hamster

Rat

3

Choosing a suitable pet

Before buying a pet there are several things to consider. Can you pay for its upkeep? Do you have time to feed it, clean it and play with it – even after the novelty has worn off? This is the only way to make it really tame. Remember also that someone will have to look after your pet whenever you go away.

You must plan how much room you will be able to give your animal. Will you house it outdoors, or is there room for it inside? Be sure that the place you choose is free of draughts, for small animals are liable to die of chills if kept in draughts.

You must be sure what kind of animal you want. Is it to be a brightly coloured, noisy bird; or a mammal, quieter and possibly not really active till late in the evening?

When you come to buy your pet, make sure you get a young animal, as it will get used to you more easily than an older one. Always choose one in good condition.

When choosing a pet look for signs of ill health. For example, avoid a budgie (above) that has ruffled feathers.

Choose an animal that is alert, lively and active with glossy fur and bright eyes, like this mouse (right). Never buy one which looks bedraggled or shivery, or which is sitting away from the others taking no notice of things. It is probably ill, and you might not be able to cure it.

General care of pets

Animals must have cages big enough for them to move about in freely. Some will also need dark, snug boxes to sleep in. Mammals like a soft, absorbent covering on the cage floor, such as sawdust. Birds need special grit scattered on the floor; they swallow some of this to help their digestion.

Cages should be cleaned regularly, but don't disturb the sleeping place more than once a week. Each month, wash the cage out well, but make sure it is quite dry before your pet goes back inside.

Most small animals will make nests to sleep in, like this hamster (above). Give them hay, straw or dry grass for their bedding.

Handle your pet often so it becomes really tame. Begin by getting it to eat from your hand (right). Don't try to pick it up until it trusts you.

Feed your pet every day, but don't give it too much; an overweight animal is not a healthy one. You can buy food specially prepared for your kind of animal in pet shops. It will also need plenty of fresh water.

A word of warning: most small pets breed rapidly. Before you put males and females together, be sure you want to keep the young. Several females should live happily together, but males may fight. Hamsters, however, must always be kept alone. If put together, they fight fiercely.

7

Pet rats

To pick up a rat, hold it gently but firmly round its middle with one hand. When it is off the ground, support its feet with the other hand.

Rats need large, strong cages, at least 75cm by 45cm and a good 45cm high, with separate sleeping quarters. They are intelligent animals and good at escaping from poorly made cages, so be warned! Like mice, rats need plenty of exercise. Their cages should have lots of ladders and branches to climb on, and an exercise wheel, if you can find one big enough. When your rats are very tame, you should let them out for a run, but keep a watchful eye on them.

Rats' main food is grain and cereals. They will also need some fruit or greenstuff, like chickweed, and food to gnaw, like nuts.

Handle your rats frequently so they learn to trust you, but always be gentle and move carefully. If you frighten them, then like all small pets they will bite.

Hooded rat

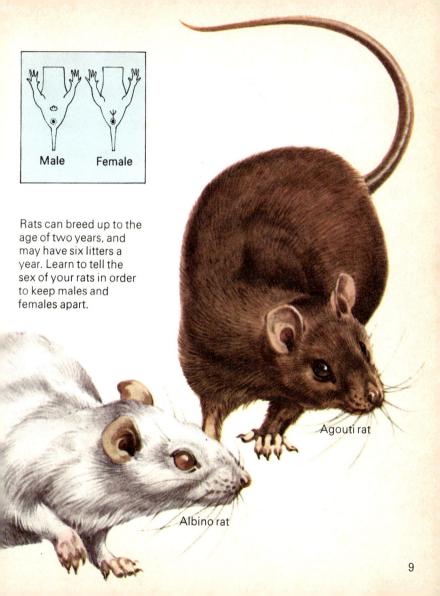

Male Female

Rats can breed up to the age of two years, and may have six litters a year. Learn to tell the sex of your rats in order to keep males and females apart.

Agouti rat

Albino rat

9

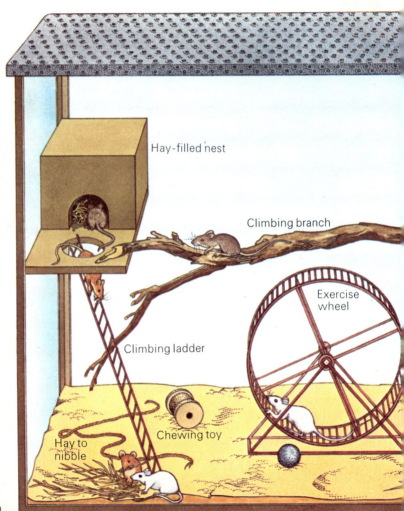

Hay-filled nest

Climbing branch

Exercise wheel

Climbing ladder

Chewing toy

Hay to nibble

Water supply

Food bowl

Mice

There are over 70 varieties of mice, and they are more popular pets than rats. A cage 46cm x 25cm x 30cm is quite big enough for a small family. A converted aquarium (like the one left) is ideal. Like rats, mice will need a hay-filled box for their sleeping quarters. Make sure you clean the cage out every day or it will begin to smell.

Mice are active little creatures and like to have something to climb on – a piece of apple tree branch is good if you can get it. They also enjoy running in exercise wheels and climbing ladders. Cotton reels and old corks make good 'toys' for them to chew.

Mice eat the same things as rats only in smaller quantities. Never give them any kind of meat or cheese as this will make them smell strongly. Do remove any stale food from the cage as it may be bad for them. Mice also like to nibble the hay in their sleeping quarters.

The proper way to pick up a mouse is to take hold of it near the base of its tail, and lift it gently on to your hand. When mice become really tame they will walk on to your hand — without even the encouragement of a titbit. As with all small animals, mice should be handled gently.

11

Hamsters

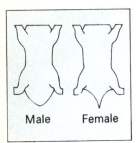

Male   Female

It is quite easy to tell male and female hamsters apart. Look at their undersides ; the end of a male's body is rounded and you cannot usually see its tail. A female's body seems to end in a point for her tail is clearly visible.

All the pet hamsters you see today come from a single family discovered in Syria in 1930. They are very clean animals and, unlike mice, will not smell unless sadly neglected. They will soon learn to use a sanitary jar placed on its side in their cage.

An upturned flower pot makes an ideal den and gives them all the privacy they need. Here they will make a nest and also store their food. Hamsters have a habit of taking all the food from their bowls and carrying it to their own private larders. As they are nocturnal (they move about at night), you should feed them only in the evening.

Hamsters are solitary creatures. If not kept apart, they will always fight each other. If you want them to breed, put the female into the male's cage for a short period every evening until they mate. Afterwards, separate them again. Baby hamsters can be kept together until about five weeks old.

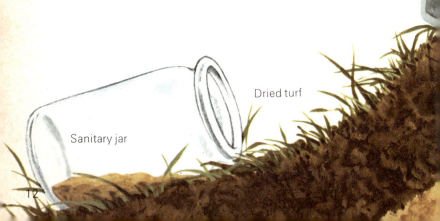

Dried turf

Sanitary jar

Exercise wheel

Flower pot den

Entrance pipe

Nest with young

Peat moss

Food store

13

14

Gerbils

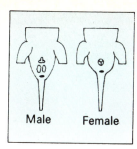

Male   Female

Gerbils are unusual among rodents in that they mate for life. A pair of them may be kept together and you will not need to remove the male after the young are born. Both parents help to look after the litter.

Gerbils come from the deserts of Central and Northern Asia and are much hardier animals than hamsters. They are active creatures and very curious. They love climbing, jumping and digging. Given a big enough cage, with a deep layer of garden peat on the floor, they will construct burrows, just as they do in the wild. In a smaller cage, you can make artificial burrows for them with bits of pipe, or the centres of kitchen paper rolls (below). They enjoy squeezing through these, although their sharp teeth will soon shred even the toughest cardboard.

Gerbils produce little urine and do not smell. So, their cages do not need cleaning as often as most pets. For their basic food give them prepared hamster or rabbit food. They also love fruit and vegetables.

Gerbils should be kept in pairs. If you don't wish to breed them, keep two females.

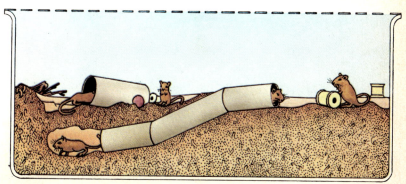

Guinea pigs

Guinea pigs, or cavies, came originally from South America. The three main types (right) are the Short-haired, the rough-coated Abyssinian, and the long-haired Peruvian. They come in many colours.

Guinea pigs are quite hardy, but need to be protected from damp, draughts and extreme cold. A simple wired-in run (below) is fine for the summer, but it must have a covered area to give them shade and protection from rain. In winter they should be kept inside.

Give them dry grass, hay or straw for bedding. Don't use wood, wool or paper as these may make the animals ill if they chew them. Their basic diet is cereals, but they need fresh fruit and green food as well. They should have plenty of fresh water.

You can keep several females, called sows, together; but never put more than one male, or boar, in a pen with them.

Guinea pigs rarely bite unless roughly handled. To pick them up, put one hand on their shoulders and support them with your other hand, or cradle them.

Shelter

Open-air run

All guinea pigs need to be groomed regularly. Short-haired ones (top right) should be brushed gently with a soft hairbrush.

Abyssinian guinea pigs (middle right) have wiry hair that grows in clusters called 'rosettes' These animals are best groomed with a toothbrush.

It is important to brush Peruvian guinea pigs often (bottom right), otherwise their fur will get tangled and matted. Brush outwards from a centre parting using a stiff brush.

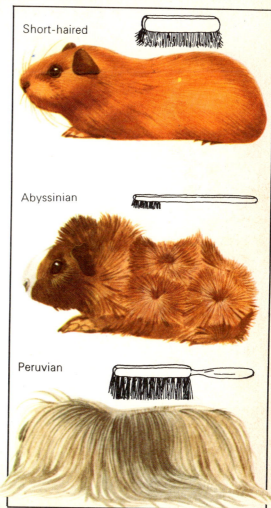

Short-haired

Abyssinian

Peruvian

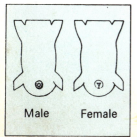

Male   Female

Rabbits

Rabbits come in all sizes. The tiny Netherland Dwarf, for example, weighs less than a kilogram, while the huge New Zealand White may be as heavy as eight kilos. There are also long and short-haired kinds.

Rabbits should be kept outdoors. They need big hutches – at least 100cm x 75cm. As they like to sit up and stand on their hind legs, the hutches have to be as high as 75cm. At one end, there should be a sleeping box with a hole big enough for the rabbits to squeeze through. Your pets will be healthier with exercise, so give them a big, wire-fenced pen to run in.

Rabbits should have two meals a day; a dry one in the morning and one of green vegetables and roots in the evening. They also need lots of fresh water and hay.

Never pick a rabbit up by its ears. To lift one, hold it by the loose fur at the scruff of its neck. Support the hind legs with your other hand. Your grip should be gentle but firm.

Himalayan

Angora

Netherland Dwarf

18

Rabbits need dark hay-lined dens at one end of their hutch where they can go and sleep. The females will also use the hay to build nests for their young.

Hay

Wire mesh

Lop

New Zealand White

Tortoises

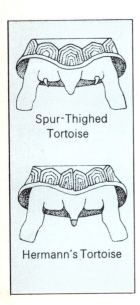

Spur-Thighed
Tortoise

Hermann's Tortoise

In the wild, tortoises mostly live in groups. So it is better to buy a pair, as a single tortoise may start roaming in search of a mate. Two popular kinds are shown left.

Make a pen for your pets in the garden. It need not be very large, but should have a box in which they can shelter. A baking tin sunk in the ground makes an ideal pool where they can drink and bathe. When drinking, tortoises put their heads under water and stay that way for a long time without coming up for air. They eat soft vegetation, like dandelions, and fruit.

If you give your pet the free run of the garden, paint your name and phone number on the shell. Never paint the shell all over, as this can harm the animal.

At the end of summer, a tortoise becomes sluggish and refuses to eat. This means it is ready to sleep (hibernate) for the winter.

Hibernating box

Earth, hay and dead leaves

When your tortoise is ready to hibernate, put it in a box (a tea chest is fine) in a frost-free place like a garage. The box should contain some earth, but mostly soft hay and leaves. The tortoise will burrow down and go into a deep sleep' till spring. All this time it will need no food or water. About March, check if it is waking up. If its eyes are gummed up, bathe them with warm water or eye lotion.

Normal Grey
Pied cock

Lace Wing hen

Normal
Green cock

Opaline Sky
Blue cock

22

Budgerigars

Albino hen

Budgerigars come from Australia. In the wild they are green, but since being kept as pets, many colours have been bred.

If you have several budgies, the best way to keep them is in a flight cage in the garden. Birds kept in indoor cages need exercise too. Once they are tame, let them out regularly to fly around the room. Before you do, remember to shut all doors and windows, and keep dogs and cats out.

Budgies eat bird-seed, and a little fresh green food helps keep them in top condition, but do remove any stale remains. Grit is vital for their digestion and should be spread on the bottom of the cage.

You can tell male budgies (cocks) from females (hens) by the colour of the cere – the small ridge above the beak. On cocks it is blue, on hens buff. Generally, cocks make better pets; they are easier to tame and learn to talk readily.

Budgies love to play with 'toys' hung in their cage, especially if kept alone. They will treat their reflection in a mirror as if it were another bird. Sprays of millet make good treats, and cuttlefish pieces for them to nibble keep their beaks trim.

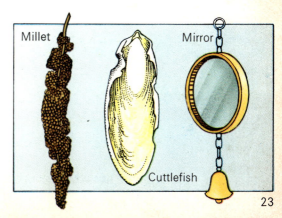

Millet

Mirror

Cuttlefish

Pintailed Whydah

St. Helena
Waxbill

Java Sparrow

Red-Crested
Cardinal

Border Canary

Zebra Finch

24

Canaries and finches

Most kinds of finches can be kept together provided you have a large enough cage; but there are some exceptions. Cardinals, being larger than most finches, tend to bully the smaller birds and ought to be kept apart. Pintailed Whydahs should only be put with birds their own size or larger.

Although most finches come from the tropics, they can live in outdoor cages as long as these have a snug, draught-proof shelter in them. Birds kept this way are often healthier than those kept in indoor cages because they get more exercise; but they do not become so tame. The perches in your cage should be different sizes to help keep the birds' feet from getting stiff.

Canaries, after budgies, are the most popular bird pets. Like all finches, they are seedeaters. Give them also a little fresh food, such as dandelion or lettuce, and let them have grit and cuttlefish too.

Breeding finches in captivity is difficult. Consult an expert before you try it. Finches need a special diet, plenty of space and a dark, cosy nesting box before they will lay eggs and raise young (above).

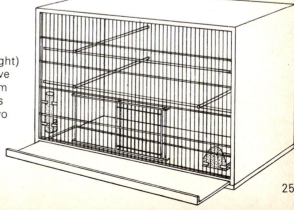

You can keep a pet canary in your living room without extra heat, but its cage (right) must be closed on five sides to shelter it from draughts. A cage this size is suitable for two birds at most.

Oranda

Swordtail

Fantail

Celestial

26

Goldfish

Goldfish live happily in unheated tanks in a light spot but out of direct sunlight. They should never be kept in a bowl, but in an aquarium with a layer of gravel on the bottom. In it, you should place Canadian pondweed and similar plants. These give the fish more natural surroundings and release oxygen into the water for them to breathe. A tank that is well stocked with plants needs little care, though you will have to clean dead matter off the bottom and scrape the sides to remove any algae growing there.

Goldfish are easy to feed. Prepared fish-food is best, but breadcrumbs, worms and small insects make a good change from their normal diet.

Common goldfish may live for 25 years, but fancy ones live less long. Although they can't be handled, or show affection the way birds or mammals do, goldfish may grow tame enough to feed from your fingers.

Veiltail

Shubunkin

Tropical fish

Many kinds of beautiful, brilliantly coloured tropical fish can live together peacefully in the same aquarium. Ask your dealer for advice about which ones to buy, for some are aggressive and will make life impossible for other fish. Gouramis, for example, can be bullies, and Angel Fish should not be kept with very small fish. Black Mollies, Zebra Fish and Tetras go well together, as do Barbs, though these may sometimes try to nip the fins of other fish.

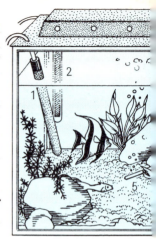

Tropical fish need less oxygen and space than coldwater fish. You can keep more of them in a standard-sized aquarium than would be possible if you had goldfish.

Kissing Gouramis

Cardinal Tetra

Cherry Barb

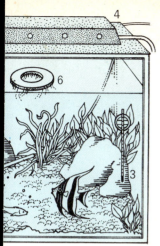

Unlike coldwater fish, tropical fish must have a certain amount of fairly expensive equipment in their aquaria. You will need a heater (1) and a thermostat (2) so the water stays at the right temperature, and a thermometer (3) to keep a check. If you do not have a light place for the aquarium, you will have to install a light box (4) above it. If the water is stocked with a large number of fish, the plants may not provide enough oxygen. The fish will come to the surface gasping for air. You will need an aerator (5) to correct the problem. Also use a feeding ring (6) to keep fish food from drifting all around the tank.

Angel Fish

Black Molly

Zebra Fish

Wild 'pets'

Even when you cannot keep pets, you can often make friends with wild creatures. Once they learn that you will not harm them, they may become very tame. Hedgehogs, which live in parks and gardens, can be enticed with a saucer of bread and milk (below). They will turn up at night to claim their treat, and will repay your hospitality by eating pests like slugs, snails and grubs.

If you have a small garden, or even a balcony or window ledge, you can attract all kinds of birds with a bird table (right). It should be strongly built and placed where cats cannot get at the birds.

Birds will eat kitchen scraps like bacon rinds and bread crusts as well as bird-seed. You should also put out a shallow water bowl for them to drink and bathe in.

Exotic pets

Think twice before buying exotic pets, no matter how appealing they are. Often they come from distant lands and need a great deal of attention and expert care if they are to survive in captivity. Trapping and transporting such animals can also involve great cruelty. For every exotic pet you see in a shop, many more have died along the way before getting there. What is more, many animals which were common in the wild only a few years ago are now becoming rare because of being taken for the pet trade.

On the whole, it is best to steer clear of exotic pets. Although you may like them, will your family share those feelings when you bring home a monkey or a snake?

However, if you do want to try your hand at keeping unusual pets, some of the best are the painted terrapins shown below. Even so, be sure you know what you are doing before you buy any.

Painted Terrapins